Safe in a Storm

James Carter

Explorer Challenge

Find out which country you would see this in ...

OXFORD
UNIVERSITY PRESS

Contents

What Is Weather?

Weather is everywhere in the world. It is happening all of the time. Weather is what it is like outside.

Weather **affects** our lives in many ways.

Weather affects where we live.

Weather affects what we wear.

Weather affects how we travel.

The weather might be sunshine or rain, clouds or wind, snow or fog.

Everyday Weather

Different places in the world have their own everyday weather.

This city in the United States of America is the sunniest place in the world.

This village in India has more rain than any other place.

traditional knup (say *ka-noop*) umbrella made from bamboo and giant leaves

The coldest temperature ever recorded was in the Antarctic. Both the Arctic and the Antarctic are always cold and icy.

Around the middle of the earth, by the **equator**, it is often hot and rainy.

equator

What Makes Weather?

We get heat and light from the sun. The sun heats both the Earth and the air. When warm and cold air meet, air moves around as wind.

heat and light from the sun

warm air

cold air

warm air

cold air

Wind helps to create different types of weather. It affects how clouds are formed, and it moves the clouds and the rain from place to place.

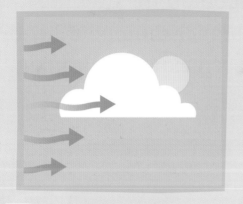

Wind moving the cloud nearer the sun

Wind moving the cloud away from the sun

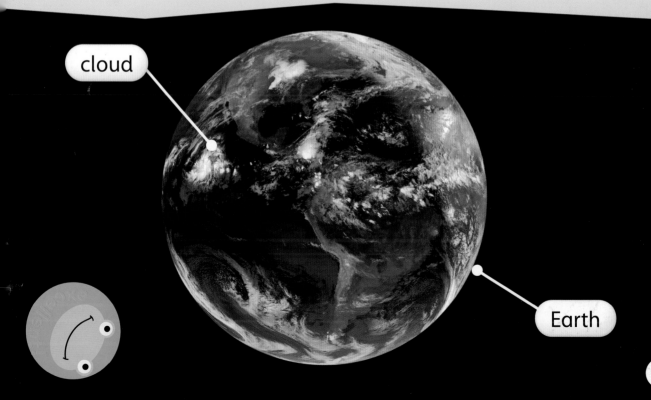

cloud

Earth

What Is Extreme Weather?

Has the wind nearly blown you off the ground?
Have you seen **snowdrifts** higher than your head?
If you have, you may have seen extreme weather.
It can be sudden and wild.

Extreme weather is different to everyday weather. It can cause big problems.

Floods

Sometimes, when rain falls for many days or weeks, large amounts of water can **overflow** on to land that is usually dry. These are called floods.

A flood in India

When floods come quickly and with little warning, they are called flash floods. They are caused by very heavy rainfall or even quickly melting snow or ice.

A flash flood in England

Keeping Safe in Floods

Some people choose to live in houses that will not flood easily.

This house can float on the water.

This house has stilts.

Hurricanes

A hurricane is a massive storm that forms out at sea over warm waters. Hurricanes can be hundreds of kilometres wide and can travel at very high speeds.

A hurricane in Mexico

From above, a hurricane looks like a swirling, giant cloud. It can have a gap in the centre known as the 'eye'.

the eye

This photograph of a hurricane has been taken from space.

Keeping Safe in Hurricanes

Some places have a 'hurricane season': a time of the year when hurricanes happen fairly often.

Hurricanes can uproot trees.

People who live in these places may use hurricane shutters to protect their homes. Shutters can be made from metal or wood, and help to stop windows smashing in heavy storms.

Blizzards

When powerful winds blow with many billions of snowflakes, you have a huge snowstorm known as a blizzard.

It is extremely cold in a blizzard, and it can be hard to see anything at all.

Blizzards can block roads.

Keeping Safe in Blizzards

Blizzards can last from a few hours to several days. The strong winds of a blizzard can create high snowdrifts.

Blizzards can form snowdrifts over three metres high.

Special winter tyres and snow chains can stop cars skidding in the snow and ice. People dress warmly when they go out in this weather. They may keep extra food at home in case it is difficult to go out.

Getting ready for heavy snow

Thunderstorms

A thunderstorm, or electrical storm, is a storm with thunder and lightning. Lightning is a hot flash of bright light which bursts from the sky. It is caused by electricity in the clouds.

Thunder is the sound that lightning makes. It can be a sudden clap or a long rumble.

These clouds tell us a thunderstorm may be coming.

Keeping Safe in Thunderstorms

Buildings often have metal rods which take the lightning safely to the ground.

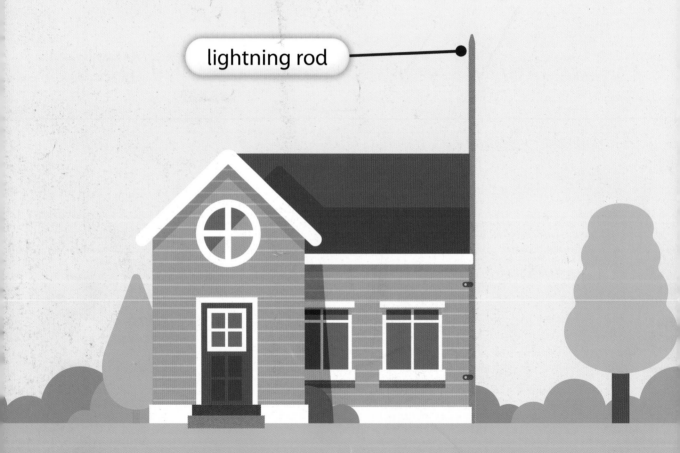

lightning rod

If you hear thunder, it is best to head indoors.

Lightning over a city in Australia

Weirdest Weather Ever!

Ever heard someone say "it's raining cats and dogs"? They just mean that it's raining hard – cats and dogs aren't actually falling from the clouds. Yet sometimes strange things *do* fall out of the sky.

Hail is balls of frozen rain. Hailstones are usually smaller than peas ...

... but this hailstone is as big as a golf ball!

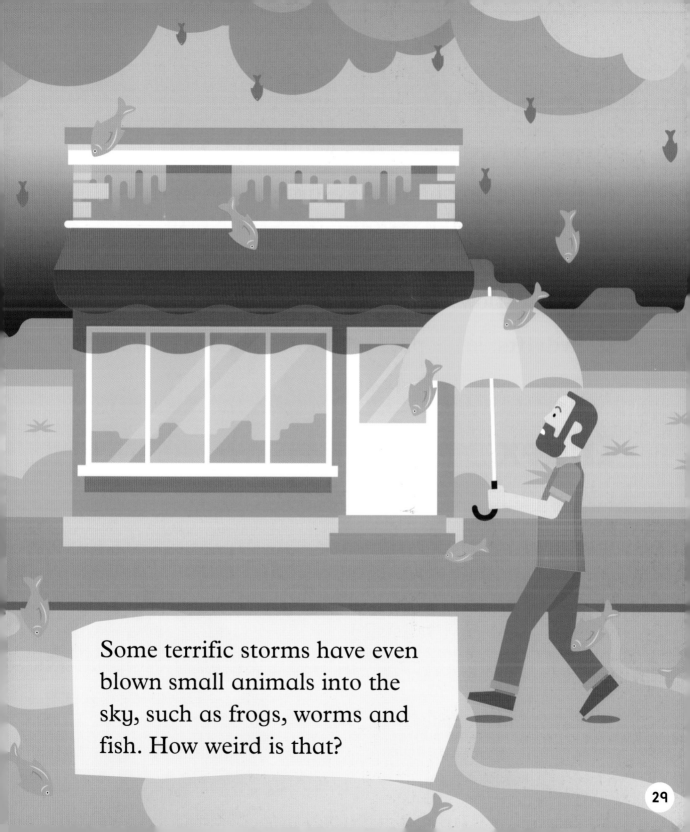

Some terrific storms have even blown small animals into the sky, such as frogs, worms and fish. How weird is that?

Glossary

affects: influences, makes a difference to

equator: an imaginary line around the Earth at an equal distance from the North and South Poles

overflow: flow over the edges of something

snowdrifts: large piles of snow made by the wind

Index

Look Back, Explorers

Where is the sunniest place in the world?

What is a blizzard?

What's the difference between a flood and a flash flood?

Why do you think a house that can float on water will not flood easily?

Thunder is described as sounding like 'a sudden clap or a long rumble'. What other descriptions of the sound can you think of?

Did you find out which country you would see this in?

Explorer Challenge: India (page 6)

What's Next, Explorers?

Now you've read about some extreme weather, find out what happens to Biff, Chip and Kipper in a thunderstorm ...

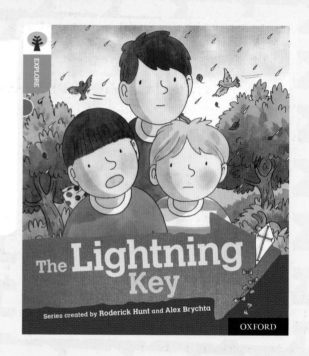

The Lightning Key

Series created by Roderick Hunt and Alex Brychta

OXFORD

Explorer Challenge
for *The Lightning Key*

Find out what happens to the hat in the storm ...